Fannie Lou Hamer

Fighting for the Rights of Others

Dona Herweck Rice

Reader Consultants

Cheryl Norman Lane, M.A.Ed.
Classroom Teacher
Chino Valley Unified School District

Jennifer M. Lopez, M.S.Ed., NBCT
Teacher Specialist—History/Social Studies
Norfolk Public Schools

iCivics Consultants

Emma Humphries, Ph.D.
Chief Education Officer

Taylor Davis, M.T.
Director of Curriculum and Content

Natacha Scott, MAT
Director of Educator Engagement

Publishing Credits

Rachelle Cracchiolo, M.S.Ed., *Publisher*
Emily R. Smith, M.A.Ed., *VP of Content Development*
Véronique Bos, *Creative Director*
Dona Herweck Rice, *Senior Content Manager*
Dani Neiley, *Associate Editor*
Fabiola Sepulveda, *Series Designer*
Chris Vallo, *Illustrator, pages 6–9*

Image Credits: front cover, p1, p5, p17, p22 courtesy of the Alabama Department of Archives and History. Photo by Jim Peppler; p3, p11, p13 (bottom) New York Public Library; p4 AP Photo/William J. Smith; pp6–9 Chris Vallo; p10 Library of Congress [LC-USF33-030569-M5]; p12, p13 (top) Everett Collection/Newscom; p14 Everett Historical/Shutterstock; p15 Maria Varela; p16 Tiago Fernandez/iStock; p18 NY Daily News via Getty Images; p19, p20, p25 Bettmann/Getty Images; p21, p24 (top) Mississippi Department of Archives and History; p23 courtesy Jean Holzschuh Sweet Estate; p24 (bottom) Federal Bureau of Investigation; p26 Getty Images/Afro Newspaper/Gado; p27 Library of Congress [LC-DIG-ppmsc-01267]; p28 Zuma Press/Newscom; p29 (top) Mississippi Development Authority via Flickr; p29 (bottom) Getty Images/Bettmann; p31 Chillin662 via Wikicommons; all other photos by iStock and/or Shutterstock

Library of Congress Cataloging-in-Publication Data

Names: Rice, Dona, author.
Title: Fannie Lou Hamer : fighting for the rights of others / Dona Herweck Rice.
Other titles: Fighting for the rights of others
Description: Huntington Beach, CA : Teacher Created Materials, [2021] |
Series: iCivics reader | Includes index. | Audience: Grades 4-6 | Summary: "Fannie Lou Hamer was born into hardship. She used the challenges in her life to drive her passion for change. She led the way toward a more just future. And her music inspired countless others to join the fight with her,"-- Provided by publisher.
Identifiers: LCCN 2020016299 (print) | LCCN 2020016300 (ebook) | ISBN 9781087605128 (paperback) | ISBN 9781087619361 (ebook)
Subjects: LCSH: Hamer, Fannie Lou--Juvenile literature. | African American women civil rights workers--Biography--Juvenile literature. | African Americans--Biography--Juvenile literature. | Civil rights workers--United States--Biography--Juvenile literature. | African Americans--Civil rights--History--20th century--Juvenile literature. | Civil rights movements--United States--History--20th century--Juvenile literature. | African Americans--Civil rights--Mississippi--History--20th century--Juvenile literature. | Civil rights movements--Mississippi--History--20th century--Juvenile literature. | Mississippi--Race relations Juvenile literature.
Classification: LCC E185.97.H35 R53 2022 (print) | LCC E185.97.H35 (ebook) | DDC 323.092 [B]--dc23
LC record available at https://lccn.loc.gov/2020016299
LC ebook record available at https://lccn.loc.gov/2020016300

TCM Teacher Created Materials
5482 Argosy Avenue
Huntington Beach, CA 92649
www.tcmpub.com

ISBN 978-1-0876-0512-8

Table of Contents

Inspiration

Fannie Lou Hamer was not born with a lot. In fact, she lived her whole life with little. But what she gave the world is far beyond what she had. She gave her spirit and her fight to make a better world, and she used her voice to lead others from injustice to civil rights for all. Despite everything she suffered, she fought on. And while she did so, she inspired countless others to do the same. Together, they changed the world for African Americans. Those changes improved the world for everyone.

She may not be as famous as other leaders of her time. But that does not change the fact that Fannie Lou Hamer is a great American hero.

Jump into Fiction

Voices Together

As Fannie Lou moved the cotton boll she had just picked from the stalk to her bag, it caught a glint of sunlight. *Pretty*, Fannie Lou thought. The fuzzy plant glowed golden like a sun-touched cloud in the sky.

Then, Fannie grimaced. She was bone-tired and her body ached. She'd been picking cotton since sunrise. And though the boll might be pretty in the light, it meant nothing but work for her. It was work she needed to help feed her family and keep a roof over their heads. But Fannie Lou was only 12 years old, and she wanted to be in school. *Life has got to be better than this*, Fannie Lou thought.

But the sun-touched cotton had inspired something in Fannie Lou. Just like the clouds in the sky tipped with golden light, it made her think of the heavens. And those thoughts put a song in her heart. Soon, the song was on her lips. Fannie Lou sang out, “Go tell it on the mountain.”

Around Fannie Lou, the other laborers picked up the song one by one. Their voices joined, building stronger and stronger. The voices singing together, despite their hardships, gave Fannie Lou a new energy.

This is better, Fannie thought. *Voices singing together. Much, much better*.

And then, standing straight and tall, Fannie Lou said out loud and strong, "I'm going to remember that."

And she did.

Back to Nonfiction

Growing Up

Fannie Lou Hamer was born as Fannie Lou Townsend in 1917. Her parents were Lou Ella and James Lee Townsend. She was their twentieth and last child! The family was very poor. They were **sharecroppers** in Mississippi. The whole family worked in the cotton fields. Hamer began picking cotton all day long when she was only six years old.

The one break Hamer had was during the winter. It was then that she could go to school. She learned to read and write in her one-room schoolhouse. Most people she knew were **illiterate**. But Hamer was able to go to school through six winters. That little bit of schooling meant a lot to her.

sharecroppers in Mississippi

schoolhouse in Mississippi

Top Student

Hamer loved to read. Poetry was a favorite, and she enjoyed reciting poems aloud as well. They were like music to her ears. She was also great at spelling and shined in school spelling bees.

By the time she was 12 years old, Hamer's life had changed. She was done going to school. Her parents' health was poor, and they needed her working on the farm all the time.

Hamer had also survived a case of **polio**. This disease ruined many young people's lives. Years later, a **vaccine** would stop its spread. But when Hamer was young, polio was common. It could be deadly, and it could even **paralyze** people. One of Hamer's legs became damaged. Despite this, she was a strong worker. By age 13, she could pick about 300 pounds (about 136 kilograms) of cotton each day!

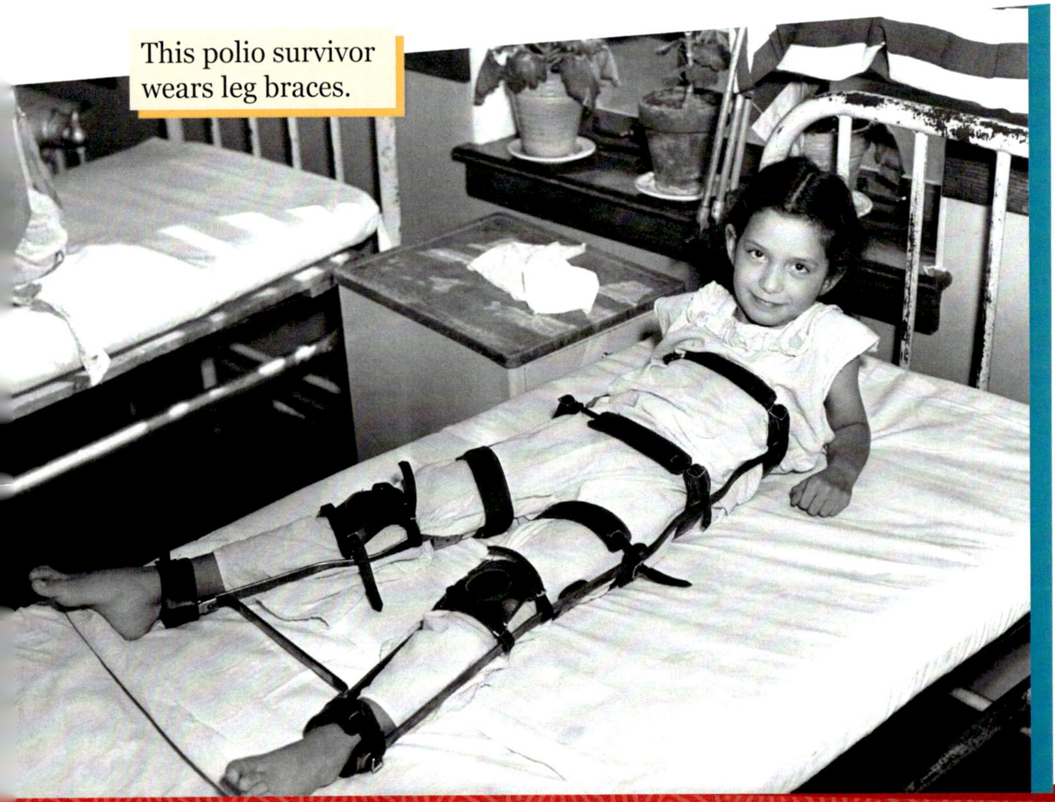

This polio survivor wears leg braces.

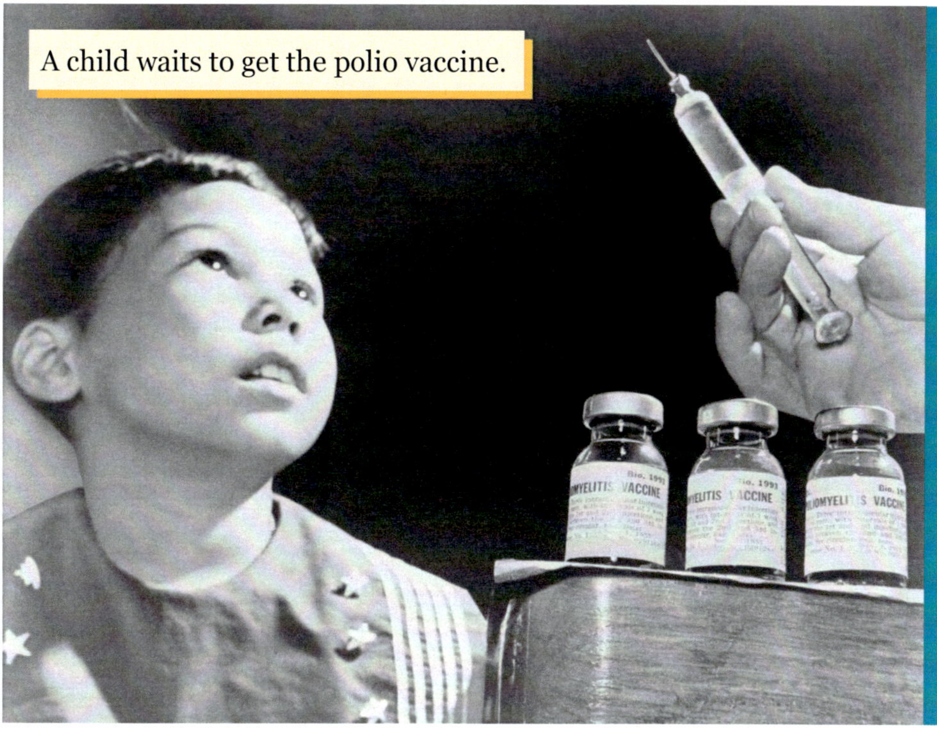

A child waits to get the polio vaccine.

Poisoned

When Hamer was young, some of her family's farm animals were poisoned. The family was certain a local white man had done it on purpose. Hamer later said this event almost ruined her family. She said, "That poison knocked us right back down flat."

Finding Her Voice

When Hamer was young, her family moved. Their new home was a few hundred miles from where Hamer was born. It neighbored a **plantation** owned by W. D. Marlow. Marlow learned that Hamer could read and write. Many of her peers were illiterate. In that time and place, education for poor Black people was rare. Marlow hired Hamer as a timekeeper. She was in charge of keeping track of hours for Marlow's workers. This new job got Hamer out of the backbreaking field work she had been doing all her life.

Think and Talk

What questions would you ask Hamer to learn more about her life so far?

Mississippi sharecroppers in 1883

On the Marlow farm, Hamer began to notice a tractor driver. His name was Perry Hamer. People called him "Pap." In time, Pap and Fannie Lou fell in love. They married in 1942.

Fannie Lou's Pap

Hamer described her husband as "a good man of few words." She said he was "steady as a rock." Despite many hard times, the couple was happy in their marriage.

Pap Hamer in 1965

The Hamers wanted kids, but it wasn't easy for them. When they had the chance to adopt a baby girl, they took it. A short while later, they adopted a second girl. The girls had families who could not care for them. The Hamers were glad to become their parents.

While the Hamers worked on their farm, Fannie Lou also took Bible classes. She valued church. Through tough times, she held tight to her faith. It gave her comfort. She also became a Bible expert. Later, she used this knowledge to support her civil rights work. She showed that civil rights were based in biblical teachings.

Hamer also used the comfort she found in church to help others. In her time, a lot of white people were violent toward Black people. **Lynchings**, shootings, and other terrorist acts were common. Hamer sang church songs to ease the pain and fear around her. She became known for her strong, passionate voice. It became her most powerful tool.

A Full House

The Hamers' two daughters were Vergie and Dorothy Jean. Vergie had been badly burned as a baby. She had been left to die, but the Hamers saved her. Dorothy Jean later had two daughters of her own. They were named Lenora and Jacqueline.

Hamer sings to a crowd in 1966.

Becoming an Activist

Hamer had known her whole life that Black people were not treated right. But two key moments in her life pushed her from awareness to **activism**.

The first event happened during a surgery that Hamer had to remove a tumor. Doctors also took out the parts of Hamer's body that let her have children. She had not agreed to this. Hamer was shocked. She was hurt and angry, too. They had **violated** her human rights. But in that day and place, there was not much she could do about it. This happened to other Black women as well. Hamer knew someone had to stand up for Black women's rights. She knew she had to speak out against this.

Black people were often attacked during this time for participating in civil rights activism.

A Violation

Hamer said that about six out of the ten Black women who went to the hospital where her surgery was done had this same thing done to them.

Hamer prepares to give a speech on human rights.

The second key event in Hamer's life happened a year later. She went to a voter meeting. Very few Black people at the time voted. Activists were trying to get people involved. Their votes mattered.

Hamer and 17 others at the meeting decided to become voters. They took a bus to the **county seat** to register to vote. But only Hamer and one other man were allowed to apply. Then, they had to pass a test. The test was not fair. It required written answers, and many Black people had not had the opportunity to learn to read or write. Both Hamer and the man failed the test.

People register to vote in 1960.

Back home, her boss, Marlow, was angry. He told Hamer she could not try to vote. When she refused, he fired her and made her move out. But Pap had to stay until the harvest was over because he needed to earn money to pay off the family's debt. He could not join the family until later.

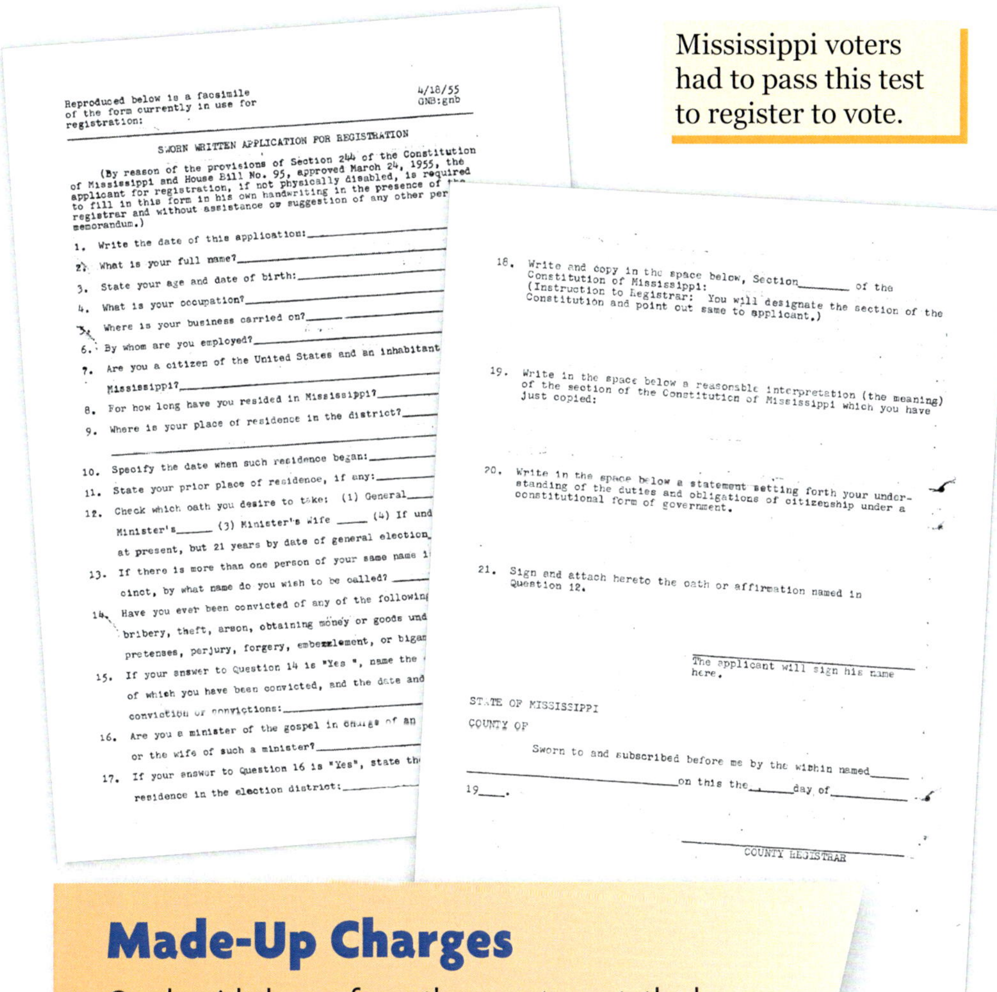

Reproduced below is a facsimile of the form currently in use for registration:

4/18/55
GNB:gnb

SWORN WRITTEN APPLICATION FOR REGISTRATION

(By reason of the provisions of Section 244 of the Constitution of Mississippi and House Bill No. 95, approved March 24, 1955, the applicant for registration, if not physically disabled, is required to fill in this form in his own handwriting in the presence of the registrar and without assistance or suggestion of any other per memorandum.)

1. Write the date of this application:
2. What is your full name?
3. State your age and date of birth:
4. What is your occupation?
5. Where is your business carried on?
6. By whom are you employed?
7. Are you a citizen of the United States and an inhabitant Mississippi?
8. For how long have you resided in Mississippi?
9. Where is your place of residence in the district?
10. Specify the date when such residence began:
11. State your prior place of residence, if any:
12. Check which oath you desire to take: (1) General Minister's (3) Minister's Wife (4) If und at present, but 21 years by date of general election
13. If there is more than one person of your same name i cinct, by what name do you wish to be called?
14. Have you ever been convicted of any of the followin bribery, theft, arson, obtaining money or goods und pretenses, perjury, forgery, embezzlement, or bigam
15. If your answer to Question 14 is "Yes", name the of which you have been convicted, and the date and conviction or convictions:
16. Are you a minister of the gospel in charge of an or the wife of such a minister?
17. If your answer to Question 16 is "Yes", state th residence in the election district:

18. Write and copy in the space below, Section ____ of the Constitution of Mississippi: (Instruction to Registrar: You will designate the section of the Constitution and point out same to applicant.)

19. Write in the space below a reasonable interpretation (the meaning) of the section of the Constitution of Mississippi which you have just copied:

20. Write in the space below a statement setting forth your understanding of the duties and obligations of citizenship under a constitutional form of government.

21. Sign and attach hereto the oath or affirmation named in Question 12.

The applicant will sign his name here.

STATE OF MISSISSIPPI
COUNTY OF

Sworn to and subscribed before me by the within named ____ on this the ____ day of ____ 19__.

COUNTY REGISTRAR

Mississippi voters had to pass this test to register to vote.

Made-Up Charges

On the ride home from the county seat, the bus driver was stopped and arrested. The police said the bus was too yellow. Hamer sang to keep the passengers calm. Finally, the passengers paid the driver's **fine** so they could return home.

After Hamer and her children left Marlow's farm, they stayed with friends. While they did, Hamer kept trying to become a voter. And she kept getting turned down. People noticed her determination, though. Someone even shot at her in an attempt to stop her!

Hamer and her children moved from house to house to stay safe. But civil rights leaders saw that she was not afraid and that she would not back down. They also saw how her voice inspired people. They thought she could be a leader.

Hamer speaks to civil rights activists.

Hamer with Lenora and Jacqueline

Sadly, around this time, Hamer's first daughter, Dorothy Jean, died. She was only 22 years old. She had been very ill, and the local hospital would not treat her. Hamer was becoming a well-known activist. The hospital staff did not want an activist's child there, so they made her leave. Dorothy Jean died on the way to a second hospital. The Hamers adopted her two daughters after her death.

Powerful Woman

Hamer was a small woman. But she had a commanding voice. One of Dorothy Jean's daughters once said, "Mama was just over five feet tall. But listening to her, you would think that she was a giant."

The death of her daughter hit Hamer hard. She started going to a lot of civil rights meetings. She wanted to make life better for her granddaughters. Hamer finally won her right to vote. Then, she helped other Black people register to vote. She also worked to improve education for Black children. She helped start a new **political party**, too. Its goal was to stop unfair laws from being passed.

At one very low point, Hamer was arrested. She and other activists sat at a diner counter marked for white people only. While in jail, the guards forced Black inmates to beat Hamer and her friends. She was badly injured, and she suffered from the injuries of this beating for the rest of her life.

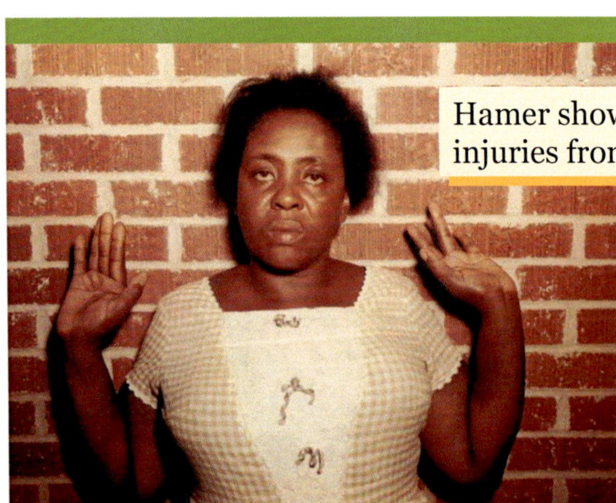

Hamer shows her injuries from jail.

Hamer speaks to politicians.

First-Class Citizen

The awful beating did not stop Hamer. She wrote that she was "determined to become a first-class citizen." Nothing else would do. She devoted her life to making sure all people had equal rights.

By 1964, a lot of people knew who Hamer was. She spoke often about equal rights. She had become famous by this point. The Democratic Party asked her to give a speech at the Democratic National Convention. This was a huge honor! Millions of people would be watching. They would hear Hamer's words.

But there was a problem. Lyndon Johnson was the Democrats' choice for president. He did not want her to appear on TV. He tried to block her speech by giving his own at the same time and drawing the attention to him. But his plan did not work. TV stations aired Hamer's speech later that night. Interest in Hamer's message spread like wildfire. More people than ever wanted to hear what she had to say.

Hamer being interviewed by a news reporter, 1965

Hamer at the 1964 convention

Jim Crow

Throughout the South, many laws were made to hurt Black people. These were known as Jim Crow laws. Hamer spoke out in her speech against these unfair laws. She said, "Is this America, the land of the free and the home of the brave?"

Sing On

People around the nation wanted to hear from Hamer. They celebrated her speeches and her singing. She inspired people. She was a key part of the civil rights movement. Today, her name may not be as well known as some other leaders, but her impact is strong.

Hamer received many honors in life as well as after her death. Colleges honored her with degrees, and public places were named for her. People still speak and march in her name.

Fannie Lou Hamer Civil Rights Museum

Think and Talk

Why do you think the author titled this section "Sing On"?

Fannie Lou Hamer died in 1977. Her life was cut short by cancer and the effects of her beating she experienced in prison. But her memory lives on, and her work lives on, too. Her powerful voice will be heard for generations to come.

Fannie Lou Hamer, Victoria Gray, and Annie Devine outside the U.S. Capitol

Glossary

activism—believing in mass demonstrations for political purposes

county seat—the city or town in a county where government offices are located

fine—an amount of money to be paid as a punishment

illiterate—not knowing how to read or write

lynchings—illegal acts in which people hang and kill others

paralyze—to make a person or animal unable to feel or move all or part of their body

plantation—a large area of land where crops are grown

polio—an infectious disease that can cause loss of movement in a person's body and the wasting away of muscles

political party—a group that organizes to direct or influence the government

sharecroppers—farmers who raise crops for landowners and are paid part of the money from the sale of the crops

vaccine—a substance that is usually injected that protects against a disease

violated—ignored, taken away, or interfered with

Index

Civics in Action

When people want things to be fair for everyone, they stand up to be heard. They write and give speeches to large crowds of people. They share their opinions on the topic. They support their ideas with facts, details, and reasons.

1. Think about a current social issue.
2. Write a speech to share your opinion on the topic.
3. Support your ideas with reasons and facts.
4. Make a poster or sign that people can hold up when you give your speech.